KU-166-661

Acknowledgments
The editor and publishers would like to thank Mary Haselden for her
help in selecting rhymes for this book and Sue Raffe, who wrote
Little green pea; A small green frog; Dreaming of bluebells;
Pale blue hippopotami; Granny's purple flowers;
Of all the colours under the sun and *The big grey elephant.*

British Library Cataloguing in Publication Data
Colours.
   1. Colours. For Children
   I. Chamberlain, Margaret
   535.6
   ISBN 0-7214-1177-0

First edition

Published by Ladybird Books Ltd Loughborough Leicestershire UK
Ladybird Books Inc Auburn Maine 04210 USA
Printed in England

colours

illustrated by MARGARET CHAMBERLAIN

Ladybird Books

red

I ride my little bicycle,
I ride it to the shop.
And when I see the big red light
I know that I must stop.

Two red engines standing in a row
With the carriages behind them
Waiting to go.
The engine driver takes his place,

The people all jump in,
The guard blows his whistle
And then the fun begins.
Chuff, chuff, chuffetty chuff.

"**O**ranges and lemons,"
Say the bells of St Clement's.

"You owe me five farthings,"
Say the bells of St Martin's.

"When will you pay me?"
Say the bells of Old Bailey.

"When I grow rich,"
Say the bells at Shoreditch.

"Pray, when will that be?"
Say the bells of Stepney.

"I'm sure I don't know,"
Says the great bell at Bow.

Here comes a candle
To light you to bed.
Here comes a chopper
To chop off your head.
Chip, chop, chip, chop
The last man's... head.

The autumn leaves
 have fallen down,
Fallen down, fallen down,
The wind, it came
 and blew them round
And blew them around.

Tiger in the jungle,
Tiger up a tree;
Tiger in the long grass,
You can't catch me!

yellow

I think it was the best of luck
That I was born a little duck;
With yellow socks and yellow shoes,
So I may wander where I choose.

Hurrah for Billy Bumble
Who had a big tumble!
Up he jumped,
And rubbed his bump,
And didn't even grumble.

Mix a pancake,
Stir a pancake,
Pop it in the pan.

Fry the pancake,
Toss the pancake,
Catch it if you can!

green

I am a little green pea,
In this fat pod I hide,
With seven other green peas
All sitting side by side.

When I am old and wrinkled,
I'm going to be sown;
I'll be a pea plant full of pods,
When I am fully grown.

"**W**ho's that tickling my back?"
said the wall.
"It's me," said the caterpillar,
"I'm learning to crawl."

Inside some jelly in a pond
There was a little egg.
One day it grew a wiggly tail
And then a little leg.

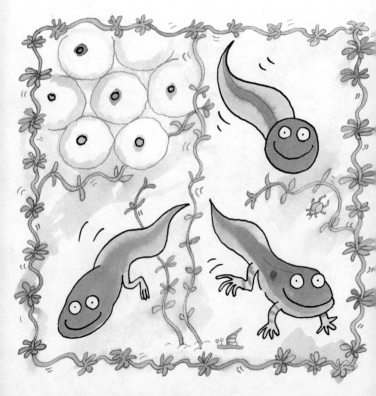

Then three more legs began to grow;
The tail became much shorter.
A small green frog
             hopped on the rocks,
Then swam across the water.

blue

The month of May is bluebell time,
And under woodland trees,
Small bells of blue
on long straight stems
Are swaying in the breeze.

My mummy says they're wild flowers,
From little bulbs they grow.
I think the fairies put them there,
A long, long time ago.

Last night, I heard the bluebells ring;
I heard their distant chimes.
Last night, I heard the fairies sing
Of long-forgotten times.

Up in the pale blue sky,
Well hidden from our sight,
Float pale blue hippopotami,
Which turn dark blue at night.

When naughty pale blue hippos
See washing out to dry,
They bounce about on big fat clouds,
And rain falls from the sky.

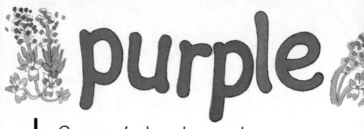

purple

In Granny's lovely garden,
Lots of purple flowers bloom;
Sometimes I pick a bunch for her
To brighten up her room.

In spring, the purple violets grow
With heart-shaped leaves, so small;
They like the dark damp patches
Beneath the mossy wall.

In summer, Granny's lavender
Just hums with buzzing bees;
Its purple flowers stand up on spikes
Above its silvery leaves.

In wintertime, plants have a rest
And hide beneath the snow;
But in some sheltered places
Buds of purple crocus show.

brown

A little rabbit on a tree
Was bobbing up and down;
His little tail was soft and white,
His two long ears were brown.

But when he heard a tiny noise,
His eyes were black as coal;
His little whiskers trembled,
And he skuttled down a hole.

A big brown owl lives in a tree,
ı a hole in the hollow tree.
isten to what he says to me,
'Tu-whit, tu-whoo!
t night I fly across the sky,
 you listen, you'll hear my cry,
u-whit, tu-whoo, tu-whit, tu-whoo!''

pink

Of all the colours under the sun
Pink must be my favourite one;
It's so easy for me to think
Of lots of nice things that are pink.

There's pink blancmange
                    and strawberry ice,
Sweet candyfloss that tastes so nice,
And blossom on the cherry tree
Raining petals down on me.

black

Big black spider
Climbing up the wall;
Never, never, never
Seems to fall.
Yet I always fall
When I climb the garden gate;
I've only got two legs
And he's got eight!

One black cat
            sitting in a tree;
Two black cats
            paddling in the sea;
Three black cats
            swinging on a swing;
Four black cats
            dancing in a ring;
Five black cats
            drinking lemonade;
Six black cats
            digging with a spade;
Seven black cats
            wearing sailor hats;
Eight black cats
            waving cricket bats;
Nine black cats
        standing on their heads;
Ten black cats
        sleeping in their beds.

grey

The elephant is large and grey,
His long trunk is his nose.
He sniffs and picks things up with it;
It looks just like a hose.

He flaps his ears to keep him cool
And shoo away the flies;
He has a tail just like a rope
And beady little eyes.

But even though he's very big
And strong, and heavy too,
He is the gentlest animal
Of all those in the zoo.

Down comes the rain!
Down comes the rain!
Beating on the roof
And on the window pane.
Flooding the gutter
And washing the street,
With splishy, splashy
                    puddles
All about my feet.
Dark are the grey clouds,
Splash it comes again,
I'm as happy as a duckling,
Paddling in the rain!

white

Brush your teeth each morning,
Brush your teeth at night;
That's the way to keep them
Strong and shining white.

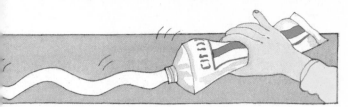

If you do this little job
Everyone will say,
"What lovely teeth you children have,
Let's see you smile today."

Softly, softly
Falling so,
This is how
The snowflakes go.

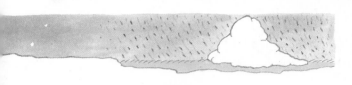

Pitter-patter, pitter-patter,
Pit pit pat,
Down go the raindrops
On my hat.